A Note to Parents

DK READERS is a compelling reading program for children designed in conjunction with leading literacy experts, including Dr. Linda Gambrell, Professor of Education at Clemson University. Dr.Gambrell has served as President of th _____ ading Association, and has recently been elected to serve as President of the International Reading Association.

Beautiful illustrations and superb full-color photographs combine with engaging, easy-to-read stories to offer a fresh approach to each subject in the series.

Each DK READER is guaranteed to capture a child's interest while developing his or her reading skills, general knowledge, and love of reading.

The five levels of DK READERS are aimed at different reading abilities, enabling you to choose the books that are exactly right for your child:

Pre-level 1: Learning to read

Level 1: Beginning to read

Level 2: Beginning to read alone

Level 3: Reading alone

Level 4: Proficient readers

The "normal" age at which a child begins to read can be anywhere from three to eight years old, so these levels are only a general guideline.

No matter which level you select, you can be sure that you are helping your child learn to read, then read to learn!

LONDON, NEW YORK, MUNICH,
MELBOURNE, AND DELHI

Editor Kate Simkins
Designer Cathy Tincknell
Design Manager Lisa Lanzarini
Project Editor Lindsay Kent
Publishing Manager Simon Beecroft
Category Publisher Alex Allan
DTP Designer Hanna Ländin
Production Nick Seston

Reading Consultant
Linda B. Gambrell

The exercises and positions in this book should only be attempted under the supervision of a qualified gymnastics teacher.

First American Edition, 2006
Published in the United States by
DK Publishing, Inc.
375 Hudson Street
New York, New York 10014

06 07 08 09 10 10 9 8 7 6 5 4 3 2 1

Published in Great Britain by Dorling Kindersley Limited

DK books are available at special discounts for bulk purchases for
sales promotion, premiums, fund-raising, or educational use.
For details contact: DK Publishing Special Markets,
375 Hudson Street, New York, NY 10014

A Cataloging-in-Publication record for this book is available
from the Library of Congress.

ISBN 13: 978-0-75662-011-0 (paperback)
ISBN 10: 0-7566-2011-2 (paperback)
ISBN 13: 978-0-75662-012-7 (hardcover)
ISBN 0-7566-2012-0 (hardcover)

Color reproduction by Media Development and Printing, UK
Printed and bound by L. Rex Printing Co. Ltd, China

The publisher would like to thank the following for their kind
permission to reproduce their photographs:
(Key: a-above; b-below/bottom; c-center; l-left; r-right; t-top)
32 Getty Images: (tr, cl); Altrendo (bl); Photonica (cr)

All other images © Dorling Kindersley
For more information see: www.dkimages.com

Discover more at

www.dk.com

DK READERS

2 BEGINNING TO READ ALONE

I Want to Be a
Gymnast

Written by Kate Simkins

DK Publishing, Inc.

Hannah and her friend Jessica
dream of being gymnasts one day.
They both go to a gymnastics class
twice a week and
they love it there.

Last week, the girls arrived
at the class after school.
They put on their leotards
in the locker rooms.

Then they ran
around the gym
to warm up.
"I hope I can
take a turn on
the beam today,"
said Hannah
to her friend.

The other girls soon arrived and
began running too.
Everyone started jumping and
hopping as well.

These exercises warmed them up so that they wouldn't injure themselves in the gym.

"Good!" said Sarah, their coach. "You should be nice and warmed up now!"

Standing tall
Learning how to stand straight and tall helps the girls look more graceful as they do gymnastics.

Next the girls did exercises to
stretch different parts of the body.
Stretching makes it easier
to do gymnastics.

Tyra was very good at forward stretches. She easily touched her toes!

Hannah stretched her feet.
Strong feet are important if you want to be a gymnast.

Then the girls did a straddle.
Their legs were stretched out wide
to the side.

"Keep your back straight and
your head up!" Sarah told them.

Tyra stretched one leg to the front and the other behind.
This is called the splits.

"I tried lots of times before I could do it," she smiled.

Pointed toes
Gymnasts should try to point their toes.
It makes their legs look longer and straighter.

The girls know they need to be strong if they want to be gymnasts.

Hannah climbed a rope to strengthen her arms.

Look at the amazing shape
Tammy made.
This shape is called a backbend and
is good for strengthening
your arms and legs.

Jessica loved
showing everyone
her somersault.

She tucked
her head and
knees in and
rolled like a ball.

Backward somersaults are harder.
Tammy learned how to do them by
using a sloping springboard
to help her.

"I want to do it again!" she said
after her first try.

"I'm worried
I'll fall over,"
said Tyra, when
it was time to do
a headstand.

"Don't worry,
I'll help you,"
promised Molly.

Handstands
All gymnasts
need to be able
to do handstands.
Molly did
a handstand
without anyone
helping her.

Molly held Tyra
as she balanced
on her hands
and head, then
straightened
her legs.

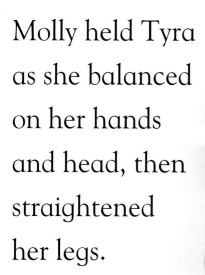

"I did it!"
Tyra smiled.

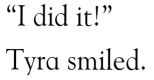

"Can I go on the beam yet?" asked Hannah.

"Maybe later," Sarah replied. "Try a cartwheel first."

The girls used a bench to learn how to do a cartwheel. They tried to keep their legs straight.

Then they tried it on the floor.
Jessica was really good.
She did four cartwheels in a row.

"It's funny being upside down!"
she laughed.

All the girls really enjoyed
jumping and leaping.
It was exciting to see how high
they could jump and
how far they could leap.

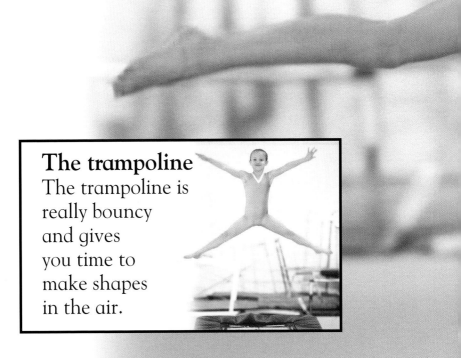

The trampoline
The trampoline is
really bouncy
and gives
you time to
make shapes
in the air.

Molly looked like she was flying as she leaped through the air.

Tammy used the trampoline to do a pike jump with straight legs.

"Who wants to try the vault?"
asked Sarah.
"I do," cried Jessica, "but
it looks really high!"

Sarah showed her how to take off
from the springboard.

When she was ready,
Jessica sprang onto
the vault.

Straddle jump

A straddle jump is like leapfrog.
Your legs are lifted high and wide above the vault.

She landed on the top and straddle jumped off again.

The girls were looking forward to
swinging on the uneven parallel bars.
First they covered their hands
in chalk to keep them from slipping.

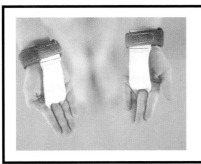

Handguards
Special covers are
worn on your hands
to stop them from
getting blisters.

Molly hung from
the higher bar.
She really enjoyed
swinging backward
and forward.

"Watch me stand on the bar!"
said Tyra as Katie helped her balance.

"Hurrah! It's the beam," cried Hannah.

Hannah showed what she could do on the beam.

She balanced on one leg and pointed her toes.

The beam
The beam is only 4 inches (10 centimeters) wide. Top gymnasts can even do jumps on the beam.

Jessica, Tammy, and Tyra walked
along the beam.
It was hard not to wobble!

The lesson was over and
the girls talked about what
they had learned.

Good Job!
After a few months of lessons,
all the girls did well enough
to get their Certificates
of Achievement.

Although the girls were very tired,
they still had enough energy
to jump in the foam pit!

Hannah and Jessica love going to the gymnastics class.

They have made lots of new friends. If they work really hard, they will get better and better.

"I hope to be a champion gymnast one day," said Hannah.

"Perhaps we will even compete in the Olympic Games!" added Jessica.

But the most important thing is that they are having lots of fun!

Gymnastics Facts

Both female and male
gymnasts take part
in competitions.
The biggest competition
is the Olympic Games.

One of the most famous
gymnasts was
Nadia Comaneci.
She was the first gymnast
to score a maximum 10
points at the Olympics.

The vault is also called
a horse.
It was first used by Roman
soldiers to practice getting
on their horses.

The uneven parallel bars
are two bars.
One is about 5 feet
(1.5 meters) high.
The other is about 7½ feet
(2.3 meters) high.

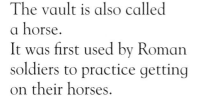